Little People, **BIG DREAMS**

STEPHEN HAWKING

Written by
Mª Isabel Sánchez Vegara

Illustrated by
Matt Hunt

Frances Lincoln
Children's Books

Little Stephen was born in Oxford, England, just as a great world war was raging. At night, he would look up at the stars and wonder what else was out there.

His parents loved science, as did Stephen and his three siblings. They all ate dinner with a knife, a fork, and the company of a good book.

Stephen was never at the top of the class, but at school everyone called him "Einstein," like the famous scientist. One day, he built a computer from clock parts and an old telephone.

Curiosity always came before schoolwork with Stephen. But still, he made it into the best universities in England: Oxford and Cambridge. He wanted to solve the mysteries of the universe.

Stephen was busy enjoying himself studying cosmology, when suddenly…

...he started dropping things and tripping for no reason.
Even his speech became hard to understand.

Doctors told him that a rare disease was paralyzing his body and he had only two more years to live. Stephen felt like the whole universe was falling down around him...

Instead of looking down at his feet,
Stephen decided to look up at the stars. Maybe
he couldn't control his body, but in order to study
the universe, all he needed was his mind.

His wife, Jane, stood by his side and gave him all the support he needed. They had three children and Stephen loved to give them rides on his wheelchair.

Stephen turned his attention to black holes, some of the strangest and most powerful objects in the galaxy. So powerful, not even light could escape from them. Or so scientists thought...

But Stephen proved that black holes were not so black after all. There was a tiny light escaping from them. It was named "Hawking radiation."

By this time, Stephen had lost his voice and found a new one with a robotic drawl. With his new voice, he dictated a book that helped the world understand the meaning of the universe.

Stephen believed that, one day, humans would cross galaxies to live on faraway planets. He celebrated his 65th birthday by taking a zero gravity ride with a team of astronauts, leaving his wheelchair for the first time in 40 years.

By becoming the most brilliant scientist of today,
little Stephen made an amazing discovery:

"However difficult life may seem, there is always
something that you can do and succeed at."

STEPHEN HAWKING

(Born 1942 • Died 2018)

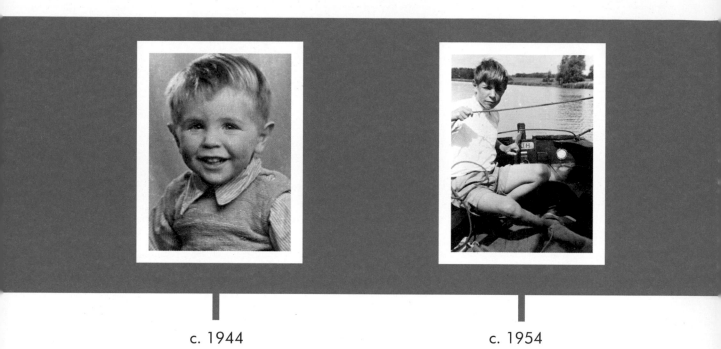

c. 1944

c. 1954

Stephen Hawking was born on January 8, 1942—exactly 300 years after the death of the astronomer Galileo. Stephen had an eccentric upbringing in a household of thinkers. Their family car was an old London taxi, his parents kept bees in the basement, and they made fireworks in the greenhouse. From an early age, Stephen used to lie in the garden, stare up at the stars, and wonder how the universe worked. But at school, he was not an exceptional student. He was always more curious about activities outside of class, like making computers and solving his own equations. Despite this, Stephen's brilliant mind took him to Oxford University to study physics, at age 17. It was during his time at Oxford that Stephen started to become clumsy. He didn't think about it too much, and kept on studying, eventually graduating with a first-class degree. It

1962   2008

was when Stephen moved to Cambridge University that he received a
diagnosis of motor neurone disease (ALS). At the age of 21, he was told
he only had a few years to live. Stephen threw himself into studying with a
new focus. He finished his PhD at Cambridge University, and later became
an esteemed professor of mathematics there. Then, while researching
and writing, Stephen came up with his black hole theory. He showed that
matter can escape from black holes in the form of radiation. He called it
"Hawking radiation." This changed the way the world thought about the
universe. Stephen lived until the age of 76, proving his doctors wrong. He
continued to study the universe, write best-selling books, and give public
speeches until he died. Stephen is remembered as a brilliant physicist who
sent shock waves through the world of modern science.

Want to find out more about **Stephen Hawking?**
Read one of these great books:

George's Secret Key to the Universe by Stephen Hawking and Lucy Hawking

All About Stephen Hawking by Chris Edwards and Amber Calderon

A Brief History of Time: From the Big Bang to Black Holes by Stephen Hawking
(advanced reading)

BOARD BOOKS

COCO CHANEL	MAYA ANGELOU	FRIDA KAHLO	AMELIA EARHART	MARIE CURIE

ISBN: 978-1-78603-245-4	ISBN: 978-1-78603-249-2	ISBN: 978-1-78603-247-8	ISBN: 978-1-78603-252-2	ISBN: 978-1-78603-253-9

ADA LOVELACE	ROSA PARKS	EMMELINE PANKHURST	AUDREY HEPBURN	ELLA FITZGERALD

ISBN:978-1-78603-259-1	ISBN: 978-1-78603-263-8	ISBN: 978-1-78603-261-4	ISBN: 978-1-78603-255-3	ISBN:978-1-78603-257-7

BOOKS & PAPER DOLLS

EMMELINE PANKHURST

ISBN: 978-1-78603-400-7

MARIE CURIE

ISBN: 978-1-78603-401-4

BOX SETS

WOMEN IN ART

ISBN: 978-1-78603-428-1

WOMEN IN SCIENCE

ISBN: 978-1-78603-429-8

Collect the Little People, BIG DREAMS series:

FRIDA KAHLO

ISBN: 978-1-84780-783-0

COCO CHANEL

ISBN: 978-1-84780-784-7

MAYA ANGELOU

ISBN: 978-1-84780-889-9

AMELIA EARHART

ISBN: 978-1-84780-888-2

AGATHA CHRISTIE

ISBN: 978-1-84780-960-5

MARIE CURIE

ISBN: 978-1-84780-962-9

ROSA PARKS

ISBN: 978-1-78603-018-4

AUDREY HEPBURN

ISBN: 978-1-78603-053-5

EMMELINE PANKHURST

ISBN: 978-1-78603-020-7

ELLA FITZGERALD

ISBN: 978-1-78603-087-0

ADA LOVELACE

ISBN: 978-1-78603-076-4

JANE AUSTEN

ISBN: 978-1-78603-120-4

GEORGIA O'KEEFFE

ISBN: 978-1-78603-122-8

HARRIET TUBMAN

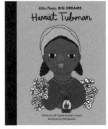

ISBN: 978-1-78603-227-0

ANNE FRANK

ISBN: 978-1-78603-229-4

MOTHER TERESA

ISBN: 978-1-78603-230-0

JOSEPHINE BAKER

ISBN: 978-1-78603-228-7

L. M. MONTGOMERY

ISBN: 978-1-78603-233-1

JANE GOODALL

ISBN: 978-1-78603-231-7

SIMONE DE BEAUVOIR

ISBN: 978-1-78603-232-4

MUHAMMAD ALI

ISBN: 978-1-78603-331-4

STEPHEN HAWKING

ISBN: 978-1-78603-333-8

Brimming with creative inspiration, how-to projects, and useful information to enrich your everyday life, Quarto Knows is a favorite destination for those pursuing their interests and passions. Visit our site and dig deeper with our books into your area of interest: Quarto Creates, Quarto Cooks, Quarto Homes, Quarto Lives, Quarto Drives, Quarto Explores, Quarto Gifts, or Quarto Kids.

The illustrations were created with digital techniques.

Set in Futura BT.

Published by Rachel Williams • Designed by Karissa Santos

Edited by Katy Flint • Production by Jenny Cundill

Manufactured in Guangdong, China CC032019

9 7 5 3 4 6 8

Photographic acknowledgments (pages 28–29, from left to right) 1. Young Stephen Hawking, c. 1944 © SWNS.com 2. 12-year-old Stephen Hawking, c. 1954 © SWNS.com 3. Stephen Hawking graduation from Oxford University, c. 1962 © SWNS.com 4. Hawking Offers Case for Space Travel on NASA Anniversary, 2008 © Handout via Getty Images